Salford
Past

at heart ♡ publications

Manchester
EveningNews

First Published in 2007 by:
At Heart Ltd, 32 Stamford Street, Altrincham,
Cheshire, WA14 1EY
in conjunction with
Manchester Evening News
1 Scott Place, Hardman Street, Manchester, M3 3RN

ISBN: 978-1-84547-165-1

Printed and bound by Bell & Bain Ltd, Glasgow

Contents

Foreword

Welcome to our look around Salford through some of the images on file at the *Manchester Evening News*. As with all our titles, this is not meant to be an academic work of any kind, though with a bit of luck we hope to entertain and inform as we dip here and there into various topics.

The book is divided into several sections, starting with *Out & About*: a look around the city of Salford and the surrounding areas of Ordsall, Pendleton, Eccles, Swinton, Kersal and Higher Broughton. The section finishes with a look at education. The earliest picture is of a class at Taylorson Street School, Salford, in about 1902 and it is worth comparing this with the pictures taken seventy or eighty years later.

The next section, *Getting About*, looks at transport: trams, buses, road and rail, from the first electric trams at Eccles to the 1984 rail crash.

Manchester Docks to Salford Quays mainly covers the 1970s, a period of decline for the Manchester Docks with the Furness Withy Group selling off no less than twenty-three ships in just twelve months. The section ends with a series of images showing the transformation from derelict dockland to today's vibrant Salford Quays area, surely one of the most successful redevelopment projects the country has seen.

The World of Work looks at industry, ranging from local collieries to Gardner diesels and Nasmyth Wilson. Finally, *This Sporting Life* includes a look at Salford and Swinton RLFCs, the Albion dog track and Manchester racecourse.

This compilation would not have been possible had it not been for the talents of photographers John Holland, Clive Cooksey, Eric Graham, Bill Batchelor, Mike Grimes, John Featherstone, John Fowler, Tony Cordt and Ian Currie, as well as journalists Barbara Duncan, Chris Stewart, David Bainton, Ann Sunderland, Neal Keeling, Chris Aspin, Beryl Jones, Gerald Brown, Jill Burdett, Peter Gardner and Keith Ward.

Out & About

• When this picture was taken in the Greengate area in February 1933, the area was already scheduled for demolition under a slum clearance scheme. Baedeker tourist guides described Salford as 'Manchester on the right bank of the Irwell, contains little to interest the stranger.'

● Christmas comes but once a year, but for these residents in Maple Street, Pendleton, it came in July 1932 when they were told they would be living rent free for several weeks after being overcharged by their landlord. Note the street lighting and the washing at the end of the street.

● Boys play with cigarette cards after the First World War.

● These shops in old Ellor Street are typical of the type that could be found in any industrialised town in the country – a chip shop and a local newsagent.

● Boot repairer and clogger's shop at the corner of Hankinson Street and Primrose Hill.

● Newsboy Ralph Brookes stands outside his father's shop in New Park Road, Salford, in May 1913. The FA Cup Final between Aston Villa and Sunderland features among the headlines as Villa's Charlie Wallace entered the history books by becoming the first player in a final to miss a penalty.

● Nashville Street in September 1960. The church in the background is St Clement's. At the time, Ordsall West Labour Party were campaigning to have the street turned into a vehicle-free 'play-street.' In 1960 there were 5,650,641 cars registered in the UK, up from 2,307,379 in 1950 and only 220,000 in 1939.

● The Ordsall redevelopment scheme as it looked in the 1960s. On the left is Ordsall Lane leading into the docks area; the lorry in the foreground is on Regent Road. Oldfield Road is off camera to the right. In the distance it is possible to make out the floodlights at Old Trafford, Trafford Park Power Station, Furness Withy House, and the massive bulk of No2 Grain Elevator at the head of No9 Dock.

● This picture was taken on 13 April 1967 and appeared in the *Manchester Evening News* seven days later with the following caption: 'Perky little lads, full of energy as they dart along the raised pavement beside tall, gnarled railings. Though present surroundings may be drab and dismal, the future is green and happy. That's the prospect that faces these children in the streets of Ordsall, when their homes are pulled down and they move to new Salford Corporation council estates.'

● With eyes bigger than their bellies, youngsters gaze through
the window of Miss Beatrice Tucker's sweetshop on the corner
of Thorpe Street, Ordsall. Soon however the sweetshop would be
nothing more than a childhood memory – the date is April 1967
and the area is scheduled for demolition.

● In July 1969 the *Manchester Evening News* broke the news that the bulldozers were crunching their way towards 'Coronation Street'. Soon Archie Street in Salford's dockland, which was featured in the opening credits of the soap and known to millions of TV viewers around the world, would be no more. One reminder of the past to be preserved was St Clement's Church with its lofty spire. When it was built in 1878 it stood among the rich green fields of Ordsall, long before the Ship Canal and docks were even thought of.

● This picture, filed in the *Manchester Evening News* archives under 'Salford Slums', was taken in February 1954.

● This is one of a series of pictures taken on 31 January 1955, recording housing conditions around the Silk Street area of the city. A five-storey mill overshadows the communal backyard of these houses in Flax Street. Note the row of outside toilets and the old mangle. By the end of 1956 Salford had rehoused over a thousand families in its new overspill estate at Little Hulton.

● The residents of Silk Street pose for the camera on 22 June 1911. Take a close look at the kids – some are bare foot, while others wear clogs. It is thought the picture was taken prior to a street party being held in celebration of the coronation of King George V.

● From the same series as the previous picture, these are the conditions the Benton family were living in at 2 Russell Street. Mrs Benton makes up a bottle for her twelve-month-old son on a gas ring. Note the ring is connected to the gas supply by a lead pipe running off an old mantle to the right of the wall mirror. A heavy guard keeps her son and solid fuel oven apart, and her washing is hanging from a drying rack hauled up to the ceiling.

● The evils of the demon drink circa 1906 are portrayed on a Sons of Temperance float courtesy of Richard Haworth & Co and the Salford Docks Commission. On the right, drink robs the man of his self respect and denies his family the necessities of life, while on the left it is made clear that abstinence will bring prosperity.

● After the Great War, neighbours in the Sandford Street area clubbed together to provide a local memorial for the men of the neighbourhood who had been killed in action, or who had died later from their wounds. In October 1961 it still stood, weather beaten but proud.

● An enumerator goes from door to door distributing forms for National Registration Day in September 1939, when occupiers had to supply details of every person staying in their homes.

● Gledhill Street, Ordsall, was pictured in August 1975 looking much as it might have done thirty years earlier for the VE-Day celebrations. It was all part of a Granada TV documentary about the year 1945.

● Queen Elizabeth II's Silver Jubilee celebrations are in full swing at Strawberry Hill, Pendleton, in June 1977 as 'Queen' Helen Taylor, aged thirteen, and a somewhat shy 'Princess' Amanda Riley, aged three, parade the cake in the general direction of photographer John Holland.

● When *Manchester Evening News* photographer Eric Graham turned up at Harvey Street, Ordsall, in July 1975, he found the place festooned with bunting and tables laid for a street party. The residents had got together to have one last fling before the demolition men moved in.

● The changing face of Salford as streets of terraced houses give way to high-rise blocks of flats, as local communities are scattered in the name of progress. This is the Ellor Street development shortly after completion. This picture was taken from Cherry Tree Court and shows (left to right) Lilac Court, Mulberry Court, Sycamore Court and Magnolia Court.

● By January 1990 Ordsall featured abandoned pubs and boarded up maisonettes – the cost of rehabilitating the area was put at £13.6million.

● Jolly boating weather. All the nostalgia of a bygone era came floating back with a rally of sixty narrow boats on the Irwell to mark the opening of a new 1.5mile navigable stretch of the river. The rally was officially launched when a small fleet loaded with representatives from Manchester, Salford and Greater Manchester councils set off from the International Marine Centre, Trafford Road, Salford, for a leisurely sail into Manchester city centre.

● Blackfriars Bridge from Victoria Bridge on 12 March 1972.

● A local historic building under threat in 1985 was Knoll House on the Salford-Manchester boundary at Strangeways. Its owners, Robinsons Removal Specialists, had applied to Salford planning committee for permission to demolish the 160-year-old structure for redevelopment.

Originally it was known as Yate's Folly. In the early 1800s Market Sted Lane in Manchester (now Market Street) was being redeveloped and businessman William Yates bought some of the half timbered frontages, had them dismantled and moved a mile up Bury New Road into what was then countryside. There he incorporated the frontages into a pair of houses, which were later converted into one, as pictured.

Mr Thomas Mills, company secretary for Robinsons said: "Although it has been a visually attractive building for so many decades, it is really a sham. It has been classified as a grade three structure of architectural and historic interest, but has never attracted the antiquarians because there is little original work left. Major repairs were carried out about ten years ago when steel girders and metal straps were inserted to support the framework. Now, making the building weatherproof and safe would involve enormous expense."

● This is the site of Salford's famous flat iron market in March 1946, with Manchester Cathedral over on the left and Blackfriars Street on the right. The market's correct name was Trinity Market but it earned its nickname from the triangular piece of ground it was held on – similar in shape to a flat iron. The market ceased in 1939 and the stallholders transferred to the new Cross Lane Market.

● A market day in September 1930. Note Joseph Luckett's horse-drawn ice cream cart.

● Forty years on from the previous picture and we have a market of a different kind. Pictured here in August 1970, Ken Dodd attracts a huge crowd to watch him perform the opening ceremony for the Great Clowes Discount Warehouse.

● As if 'Doddy' wasn't enough of an attraction, the Great Clowes Warehouse also hired Irma the elephant from Belle Vue Zoo. She is seen here making her way along Market Street in Manchester on her way to Salford.

● Salford City Shopping Centre on a wet morning in November 1971.

● The sweeping modern lines of Salford City Shopping Centre was all part of the new shopping experience.

● The Victoria Theatre was going through a rocky period in 1963 and was hanging on by a thread as a place for live entertainment. However, the *Manchester Evening News'* postbag did carry letters from readers who liked the friendly atmosphere of the staff and manager at the Vic which was as one reader put it, "very different from the 'snotty' attitude of the Opera House, impersonal atmosphere of the Palace, or clinical atmosphere of the Library Theatre."

● Chapel Street, 3 June 1975.

● Two famous Salford landmarks photographed in the 1970s are The Beehive pub as it looked on the 7 March 1974, and Poets' Corner on Lower Broughton Road as it looked on the 3 June 1975.

● In close-knit communities, local pubs and corner shops were important focal points. Here we have two Whit Lane establishments: the Elephant & Castle, and the Jubilee Inn.

● The Town Hall was built in the Grecian Revival style between 1825-27, to a design by architects Richard Lane and Francis Goodwin. Our picture of the Town Hall was taken in 1926. Lane was also responsible for designing the Town Hall at Chorlton-cum-Medlock, Bolton Exchange and St. Mary's Church in Oldham. Lane joined forces with Goodwin again to design St. Thomas' in Pendleton.

● Members of the District Works Department hoist the royal arms back to their rightful position above the entrance to the Town Hall in 1953. The recently repainted arms had not been used since before the outbreak of war in 1939.

● Firemen rescue a man trapped at the top of a 50ft tower in August 1953. They lowered him carefully to the ground in a sling – and then he got up and walked off without as much as a thank you. But nobody minded because it was an exercise held during the annual brigade inspection and the rescued man was 26-year-old fireman Richard Gregory. During the drill the brigade used a new light steel alloy escape ladder, Salford being the first to be equipped with the new piece of kit. It weighed in at just 2cwt, much lighter than the 17cwt of the traditional wheeled ladder. Apart from the weight advantage, the new ladder was also easier to handle in confined spaces.

● Salford's firemen and appliances were lined up for their annual inspection on 24 May 1957 when a call came through about a chimney fire in Bolton Road, Pendleton. But the inspection went ahead, with H.M.Inspector of Fire Brigades, Mr A.V. Thomas, praising the fifty-year-old fire station: "It is equal to any being built today." He was also impressed with the number of off-duty men who had turned up for the parade. In the picture are Mr A.V. Thomas (left), Leading Fireman H. Miles and Fireman N. Heap (wearing respirator).

● The latest addition to the City of Salford Fire Department in April 1954 was a semi-limousine bodied F.8 pump supplied by Dennis Bros of Guildford. It was powered by a 120bhp Rolls-Royce 6-cyl engine and came equipped with a Dennis 500gpm turbine pump.

● During the Blitz, brothers Derrick and Frank Corfield both drove the City of Salford turntable ladder fire engine. In December 1990 they paid a visit to see their old engine at the Museum of Transport at Boyle Street, Cheetham. Both attended the Blitz Memorial Service at Manchester Cathedral.

● Members of Broughton's Green Watch in March 1995.

● In July 1970 nurses at Salford Royal Hospital were being blamed for bandaging the leg of an "unknown soldier." For more than a week the statue of an anonymous Boer War hero had stood on his plinth sporting a bandaged leg. To reach the statue, which had stood at the junction of Oldfield Road and Chapel Street for 65 years, the pranksters would have had to scale over four foot high railings and scramble to the top of the plinth at least fifteen feet above the ground. "Of course, we cannot be sure, but it seems highly likely that this is the work of nurses at this hospital who were a little high spirited. It is in extremely bad taste," said a spokesman for the hospital.

● Salford Royal Hospital dated back to 1830 and was extended in 1911. After the NHS closed it, it was converted into apartments

● This is the gaping hole that tore into the nurses' home at Salford Royal Infirmary during the Blitz. Fourteen nurses were killed, as was the Reverend James Hussey from St Philip's Church. He was walking over to the infirmary to comfort the wounded when the bomb fell.

● One of the features of the old Hope Hospital was the bridges linking the buildings.

● This picture of the Victorian gateway at Peel Park was taken in 1935, the bunting marking the visit by King George V and Queen Mary in their silver jubilee year. The gateway was demolished before the war when it was declared unsafe due to crumbling brickwork. By the late fifties the whole site had been cleared to make way for the University of Salford. The area shown here is where the Maxwell Building was later erected. The statue seen through the gateway is of Joseph Brotherton, first MP for Salford.

● St Philip's with its unique bow-fronted porch supported on Ionic columns, is a neo-classical Greek masterpiece by architect Robert Smirke.

Royal Visit to Salford. July 14 191

Spectators in Peel Park.

● Spectators in Peel Park for the State visit of King George V and Queen Mary on 14 July 1913, to open the Technical Institute. The King had succeeded to the throne only three years before. According to the records it was a grey, drizzly day.

● Royston Futter, new head of Salford City Council's cultural services, in June 1996, with Councillor Hazel Blears among the Lowry Collection in the Peel Hall Art Gallery.

● The Art Gallery with the library on the left and the University's Peel Tower between them. Peel Tower was demolished in 1994.

● L. S. Lowry was left speechless at Salford Town Hall on 8 June 1965 when he was made a Freeman of the city. "No speech from me – I am just no good at it," said the seventy-seven year-old artist. Lowry, whose paintings of the Lancashire industrial landscape had made him famous throughout the world, received the silk scroll and wooden casket from Salford Mayor, Alderman Bertha Davis, and then listened with an amused grin on his boyish face as civic leaders paid tribute to him.

● "Travellers through Salford could have their day brightened if banking at The Crescent was turned into an attractive rock garden," Councillor Ruth Dodd told the city's recreation committee in May 1961. She added, "From time to time, very expensive floral displays are attractive for short periods, but a permanent rock garden would be there all year round and cost no more. This could be an attractive focal point of the city, but for most of the year it is just an ugly patch." Plans for 1962 already included planting 200,000 tightly packed blooms depicting the city's coat of arms, as well as the planting of 140,000 shrubs and trees on housing estates, school playing fields and in the parks. Our image shows one of the floral displays Councillor Dodd was referring to, it was also the site of the proposed rock garden.

● The same date as the previous picture. Ian Currie took this view of Broad Street. The Tower block is Spruce Court; the then modern buildings on the other side of the carriageway belong to Salford College of Technology.

● Photographer Ian Currie was out and about in March 1978 taking a number of rooftop pictures of Salford. This picture shows The Crescent, the principle trunk route out of Manchester into Salford and on to the East Lancs. The railway line arcing through the centre of the picture is the busy Liverpool-Blackpool, which brings passengers into Salford and Manchester. A limestone train, from Peak Forest near Buxton, can be seen discharging at the Hope Street stone terminal.

● Marchers set off from Salford College of Technology, where they had spent the night, before joining up with the nationwide 'Peoples march for jobs' in May 1981.

● Taken by Eric Graham in July 1984, this picture features famous landmarks, the swing bridge and the Bridgewater Canal aqueduct. It also provides us with a good view over Barton upon Irwell, Eccles, Winton, and parts of Patricroft and Eccles. Over towards the top right we can see the M60/M602 interchange.

● View over the centre of Eccles taken in October 1951. The Broadway cinema is almost in the centre of the picture, whilst the town's monument to the fallen of both world wars – standing in the middle of a traffic island - can be seen a little further over to the left. Between the two stands the Town Hall with its clock tower and multiple chimney stacks. In the top left-hand corner, St Andrew's church is just visible.

● This comparative view of Eccles close to St Andrew's Church taken in 1978 gives us an idea of how much of a swathe the M602 cuts through the town.

● The Duke of York pub
in Church Street, Eccles.

● Turning the clock back to the early years of the twentieth century, this is the Jubilee procession of the Eccles Co-operative Society making its way along Park Street, Swinton.

● At 11am on 14 October 1990 these flats at Kersal were demolished, a sign that the great social engineering schemes on the 1970s had failed. It took just eight seconds and half a ton of explosives to reduce the flats - named after the poets Browning, Jonson, Milton, Burns, Shakespeare, Keats, Chaucer and Bacon – to 50,000 tons of rubble. A huge dust cloud blocked out the sun for several minutes and when it cleared only a 90ft lift shaft – later dubbed the Leaning Tower of Kersal – remained standing. The Leeds-based firm Controlled Demolition Group undertook the job, which was worthy of a mention in the *Guinness Book of Records* as the largest number of buildings brought down in one go.

● After the demolition, residents who had been evacuated on safety grounds were allowed back into the area. The flats had been officially opened in March 1962 by the then Labour leader Hugh Gaitskell but by 1988 they had been abandoned by tenants fed up with the high levels of vandalism on the estate.

● Another building under threat of disappearing – but this time for the wrong reasons – was Kersal Cell. Occupying the site of an old religious house dating back to the twelfth century it had even withstood the ravages of the Reformation – but local youngsters were another matter. During 1989 they had repeatedly broken in to: deface a 400-year-old wall painting, dig out chunks of plasterwork dating back to the mid-1600s, destroy timberwork from the same period, and inflict substantial damage to a Jacobean staircase. The Greater Manchester Archaeological Unit was carrying out a survey and their manager, Nigel Neil, told the *Manchester Evening News*' Chris Stewart, "as a building, this is one of the most important in Greater Manchester. What is particularly saddening is the damage to the actual fabric of the building, such as the few original window frames which still remain, and damage caused to the roof is endangering the whole structure." Kersal Cell, which lay in the shadow of Agecroft Colliery, was originally a Clunic monastic cell for two monks, but was sold off after the 1536 Act of Suppression. From 1613 until about 1870 it was the Byrom family home, then a girls' boarding school and later a disco, but had been empty since about 1985. Dog patrols had been brought in to keep the kids at bay and plans were afoot to turn it into a pub and restaurant.

● An almost vehicle free Wiltshire Street, Higher Broughton, in May 1964.

● The Acme Mill and the cooling towers of Agecroft Power Station can be seen on the skyline of this picture taken by Ian Currie from the roof of Swinton Town Hall on 5 April 1978.

● Landlord Joseph Gregory stands with hands in pockets outside the Bull's Head at Walkden. The site was later occupied by the Palace Cinema.

● There were no frills about education at the beginning of the twentieth century. This picture was taken at Taylorson Street School, Salford, in about 1902. Apart from a print of Napoleon Bonaparte on his way to exile, there is little on the bleak brick walls save paint. The class notice board consists of a few nails hammered into the wall and light is supplied courtesy of flaring gas jets. Close-cropped heads weren't so much a fashion statement as a practical way of preventing the spread of vermin, and those smart stiff white collars the boys are wearing were made of rubber so they could be sponged clean.

● The boys of Salford Grammar are treated to a recital by K.A.Smith, winner of the intermediate verse and prose, 1952, at the annual speech day ceremony held at the Salford Hippodrome. The school opened in 1904, but as it lacked its own premises it was housed in the Technical College.

● Some of the first pupils on site at the new £250,000 Salford Grammar School at Claremont, Pendleton, check out the equipment in the woodwork room.

● These pictures were taken in 1960 in what was then known as the Housecraft Section of the newly opened Ordsall Secondary Modern School for Girls. The pictures were in a series titled 'Housewives of Tomorrow' and show the model flat where girls were taught how to make beds, lay the table, tidy up, and the kitchen which at the time was equipped with some of the latest labour saving equipment.

● St George's
C of E, Whit Lane, on
16 September 1971.

● A typical classroom at St George's C of E School, Pendleton, in September 1971.

● In January 1964 it was new term, new school, for the 400 pupils of Broughton High School for Girls. Workmen were still putting the finishing touches to the £300,000 building and a leaking boiler resulted in the girls moving in just two days behind schedule. The old school building, about a mile away in Bury New Road at 'Bella Vista,' the former home of the Greek consul, was to be demolished to make way for a new primary school.

● The new Cromwell Secondary School for Girls, which featured a wall mural made from ice-age pebbles excavated from the foundations, was officially opened in October 1962.

● Playtime at Garnett Street Boys' School in November 1972.

• Princess Anne on a visit to Salford in May 1982.

● This picture taken on 4 February 1988 shows a classroom at Halton Bank School, Irlam o' th' Height.

● On 23 March 1995, Ron Baybutt reported on the fundraising going on at Grosvenor Road Junior School, Swinton. The headmistress Mrs Margaret Baker had asked the children for ideas on how to raise money for charities. The children's suggestion was, 'Why not raffle somebody?' So the school held a raffle with the winning pupil becoming headmistress or headmaster for the day, and Mrs Baker taking their place as a pupil in the class. The raffle raised £130 for the Relief of Orphans Fund. Mrs Baker already knew about an orphanage in St. Petersburg, Russia, and so the children decided to send the money they had raised to the orphanage.

● In 1986 Chris Stewart reported that town planners were to defy the law and demolish the listed Ordsall Primary School building in order to avert a tragedy. The building, dating from 1884 and deemed by the Department of the Environment to be of special historical and architectural interest, was in a pitiful state, torn apart by thieves and vandals, with walls thought to be near to collapse.

Fire brigade chiefs had also informed the city council that serious fires were happening at the school at a rate of about one a fortnight and that children found in the school by firefighters could easily have been trapped there. Planners had been unable to find anyone willing to take on the property.

Furthermore, it was felt that any money spent on extra security would be a waste of time because the wreckers would still find a way in. Councillors decided to call in the bulldozers, admitting that to do so would put them in breach of the 1971 Town and Country Planning Act. The Act required the council to apply for special permission to demolish the pile from Environment Secretary Nicholas Ridley, but planning chairman Councillor Ben Wallsworth said: "The safety of the children in this residential area is uppermost in our minds, and that determined our actions. We hope the Environment Secretary understands the reasons for our decision."

● Angela Chappell, Salford City Council's community arts officer, celebrates with local Pendleton school children at the opening of the sundial made from a derelict flower bed outside shops on Cavell Way next to the Phoenix Theatre.

● In March 1993, Mayor Kenneth Murray and nine former Salford mayors sat down to a thank you dinner given by John Squires, principal of Salford University College. During the meal Mr Squires praised them for the support they had given to the university, which had become established as one of the fastest-growing higher education institutions in the country.

At the event, in no particular order, were chairman of the governors Joan Bryans and past mayors Joe Murphy, Thomas Hobbs, John Hincks, Jack Smith, Dr Joe Jaffe, Sydney Turner, Joseph Holt and Ivor Zott. Seated in the front row of our image was 'then' mayor Kenneth Murray and, at the time, the city's oldest ex-mayor, 86-year-old Thomas Francis.

● "Trust me, I'm a newspaper man. It won't hurt a bit." A *Manchester Evening News* photographer persuaded a student to strike this pose inside the first section of the new Avro wind tunnel at Salford Royal Technical College in October 1957. The cost, around £7000, was being met by Avro who were also financing the equipping of an aeronautics laboratory. The Royal College became the University of Salford in 1967.

● Continued expansion of the University of Salford in April 1967 included a boiler house whose tall metal chimney can be seen here pointing skywards. To the left of the chimney in the background stands Salford College of Technology - formerly known as Peel Park Technical College – which became Salford University College in 1992.

● Across the River Irwell, and connected to Peel Park by a new bridge, stands the partially completed Civil Engineering block, in April 1967.

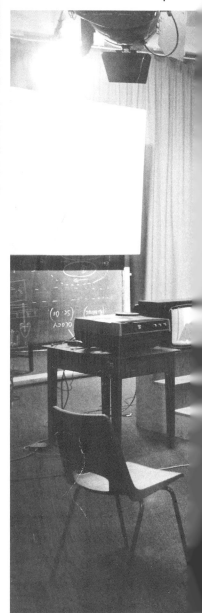

● In March 1972, Salford was the first university in Europe to install a £390 video-tape machine as an experimental teaching aid. At the time the video cassettes of recorded programmes, which ran from between twenty minutes and one hour, cost up to £75 each. As the *Manchester Evening News* reported, one of the advantages of video was that a teacher or lecturer could stop a film at any point, rewind it or hold it on any frame. Our picture shows the university television studio. In front of the cameras are Dr Aled Rhys William, unit director, and producer Susan Sayer. The video unit is on the table to the left of the picture.

● Five hundred students campaigning for longer visiting hours at Salford University halls of residence occupied the registrar's offices in The Crescent in March 1976. The Students' Union president, 27-year-old Tony Edwards, said: "The dispute over visiting hours has been going on for some years. At the moment visitors are not allowed after midnight. We want this rule abolished for weekends so that a student can have a visitor all night in his room if he wishes. We have been talking to the university authorities about this, and today we heard that the Senate have merely agreed to 'look at the possibility of lengthening the visiting hours'. We held a meeting and people felt this just wasn't good enough, so we decided to take more direct action."

● By 1979 the Japanese were world leaders in the field of electronics, yet 31-year-old electrical engineer Akiyoshi Inove came all the way to the University of Salford to further his education. After receiving his MSc in micro-electronics, Akiyoshi, accompanied by his son, Sadayoshi, aged three, chatted with Prince Phillip who was on a two-day visit to Manchester and Salford.

● Professor Michael Hampshire, professor of electronics, explains the workings of the micro-chip wiring system in a Ford Escort to Prince Phillip, watched by, left, the Vice-Chancellor, Professor J. H. Horlock, and Mr. Michael Goldstone.

● Margaret Thatcher surrounded by officials and security men arrives at Salford University in January 1982. The presence of the men in grey suits didn't stop the three hundred students protesting about Government cash cuts, by parading a black draped coffin.

Getting About

• In February 1982 tramway enthusiasts were working by night to save a unique piece of history – a clover leaf-shaped tramway intersection at the junction of Ship Corner and Regent Street, probably the last one left in the world.

The trackwork, weighing 62 tons, was being salvaged because the M602 then being built between Eccles and Cross Lane would obliterate it. At Ship Corner (the junction of Eccles New Road, Cross Lane, and Trafford Road) double sets of tram tracks went round each of the four corners, with sixteen sets of points – all automatic. In their heyday, dozens of key tram routes crossed at Ship Corner, carrying thousands of passengers to Trafford Park, Salford Docks, central Manchester, Pendleton and factories in Eccles.

The trackwork was manufactured by Hadfields of Sheffield who would lay it out in their yard, every piece numbered, so that it when it was delivered it could be slotted into place in the shortest time possible. Although it had been buried under six inches of bitumen for the best part of thirty-five years, it was found to be still in first class mechanical condition. Hadfields were so proud of this junction that it featured in their catalogue.

● This is Church Street, Eccles, in 1902 and preparation
work for the new electric tramway is taking place.

MOSES GATE

GRAY STOVE POLISH 1ᵈ & 3ᵈ

FIRST TRAM CAR ARRIVAL
AT WALKDEN JUNE 22ⁿᵈ 1906.

● The people of Walkden turned out on 22 June 1906 to see the first electric tramcar arrive.

● The junction of Cross Lane and Broad Street, Pendleton, used to be known as "Jean's Corner," because of Jean's chemist's shop. The middle-of-the-road tramway standards caused numerous accidents before they were removed.

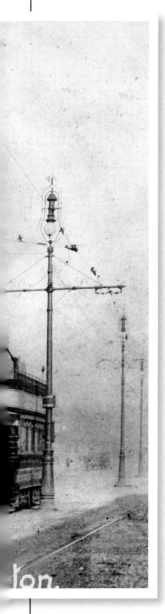

● It's the end of the line for this Salford tram. Having been sold for scrap it awaits its fate at Hyde Road Depot yard, Manchester, in June 1947. By the end of August 1946 the Salford tram fleet numbered just thirty-eight operational vehicles and twenty that were not fit for service. In January 1947 the peak-hours only service between Victoria and Cromwell Bridge via Lower Broughton Road finished, to be followed on 2 March by the Deansgate to Weaste route. Only the Deansgate and Docks circular routes remained and on 31 March, car No 350 ran the last service. The cars were taken to Hyde Road for scrapping.

● In August 1935 it was announced that Salford Transport Committee was considering acquiring a site near Victoria Bridge for use as a purpose built bus station. The proposed site covered Thomas Cook's ticket office and several buildings, including Simpole's showrooms as shown in the image.

● This photograph, dated 21 August 1937, shows work underway on the new bus station adjacent to Victoria Bridge. The picture was taken from the tower of Manchester Cathedral.

● Seen here at the Ordsall Lane terminus, Salford Corporation
bus No 457 sports a special Coronation livery used for about
five weeks during 1953.

● In October 1971, *Manchester Evening News* photographer Eric
Graham joined the 2,500 or so people who took the chance to walk along
the two miles of the unopened M602. Building the £11million dual three-
lane motorway – the first urban motorway in Lancashire – had caused major
disruption in Eccles for more than two years, though it had been completed
two months ahead of schedule. The contractors opened the motorway for
four hours and in glorious sunshine it became something of a day out as
families made the four-mile round trip from the Salford end, where there
was single lane access. The barriers were afterwards replaced to
await the official opening by county alderman W.D.Cooper, chairman of
the county highways and bridges committee. The motorway offered an
alternative to the narrow Manchester – Liverpool road through Eccles,
Patricroft and Peel Green which, for at least fifty years, had been an
accident blackspot.

● Platforms jam-packed with holiday makers were still the norm in the early 1960s – this lot were heading for North Wales.

● Opened in 1884 and closed in 1969 – even though it was making a profit of around £265,000 a year - Exchange Station is seen here in the course of demolition.

● Chapel Street and Salford Station on 20 February 1967.

● In 1979 for the first time in decades, the fine Victorian decoration stands out on the railway bridge crossing over New Bailey Street at Salford Station. Picture by Bill Batchelor.

● On 4 December 1984 a Liverpool – Scarborough express train ploughed into the back of a freight train causing a massive explosion. Our picture shows the white-hot fire engulfing the passenger train soon after the collision which left three dead and 68 injured.

● Salvage work gets underway and heavy-lifting equipment
has been brought in to lift the flame-seared rolling stock.
Picture by John Fox.

● Though the flames and smoke have gone, firefighters
take precautions by continuing to spray foam onto the
smouldering wreckage.

Manchester Docks
to
Salford Quays

• The main entrance gate to the Manchester Docks photographed on
29 November 1969.

● The Leyland Lioness came in a variety of guises. These included the Karrier charabanc of the late-1920s, the LTB1 fire engine, and the coach shown here being loaded at Manchester for export. The picture is thought to date from the 1930s.

● The Second World War brought with it increased activity at the docks and one of the knock-on effects was that the peace time facilities for seamen were soon overstretched. In April 1940 a seamen's mission was opened at 293 Oldfield Road, Salford, to take the overspill from the existing mission in Trafford Road. The new mission – formerly a girls' hostel - was for use by seamen of all nationalities visiting the port and was able to offer meals and accommodation as well as being somewhere to go for a drink and a game of dominoes. It was officially opened by the Mayor of Salford, Alderman J. A.Webb.

● No9 Dock as seen from Trafford Wharf in January 1974. *Manchester Courage* is alongside the container terminal: the nearest vessel alongside the opposite quay is Prince Line's *Spartan Prince*. Round-the-clock working enabled a 500-capacity container ship to be turned round in just 48 hours. No8 pier was equipped with a 32 ton derrick crane and could handle vessels carrying part container loads.

● An aerial view of Manchester Docks from the 1970s shows their proximity to the city centre.

● View from the bridge of *Manchester Crusade* as she loads her next cargo of containers at No9 Dock on 17 January 1972.

● A show of hands vote for a return to work at a strikers' meeting held outside the docks.

● In December 1970 the Ellerman Lines cargo-liner *City of Guildford* was one of the ships trapped in the Manchester Docks due to strike action.

● During 1974 Smith's Dock completed a pair of 12,577 ton container ships for Manchester Liners both of which went on immediate charter to the Australian Asian Express Line under the names *Asian Renown* and *Asian Reward (pictured above)*. Their names were changed by simply substituting *Asian* for *Manchester* and when the charter ended during 1978 both vessels reverted to their Manchester names. The following year *Manchester Reward* was chartered to Seatrain Lines and renamed *Seatrain Norfolk* and later *TFL Reward*, reverting back to *Manchester Reward* during 1980.

● The outbound *Lady Grania* passing
Barton Aqueduct on 15 May 1974.

● In September 1983 Salford had a new tourist attraction – the leaning Grain Elevator of No9 Dock. After weeks of demolition work, the 200ft elevator off Trafford Road had keeled over at an angle. After years of disuse, the seventy-year-old building was scheduled for demolition but contractors were forced to take a softly-softly approach rather than go for the big bang as everyone expected. Peter O'Connor, managing director of the demolition contractors explained to *MEN* journalist Paul Taylor: "This is the first phase. We had to get it away from the docks or it would have gone into the canal. If we blasted it in one go, the way some people expected, we would have flooded the whole area. We have been blasting at it for five weeks now and we expect to carry on for another two weeks." Despite the phenomenal 75 degree tilt, the reinforced concrete structure was still as solid as a rock. "We have been walking around in there and it's quite safe," said Mr O'Connor.

● By July 1984 the docks were the equivalent of a ghost town. There is not a cargo ship to be seen, and though many of the warehouses are still standing, No2 Grain Elevator has been reduced to a mound of rubble. Virtually all the dockside cranes have gone, the railway ripped up, and the hustle and bustle of what was once one of the busiest ports in the country is nothing more than memories.

● The changing face of Salford Quays in September 1989 as redevelopment gathers pace. Little now remains of former days save the former main entrance (now blocked), the dock offices, the Furness Withy House, and several cranes.

In 1910 Baedeker described the docks as 'one of the boldest modern experiments in inland navigation, which has practically placed Manchester among the principal seaports of Great Britain'.

● The latest phase in the multi-million pound redevelopment of
the Quays in June 1987 was the eighty-metre long Chandlers
Canal, the first of two costing £750,000 that would link up
the water network. All six of the Quay's water basins had been
sealed off from the Ship Canal to keep out polluted water, and
special aeration equipment was in the process of being installed
to improve water quality. A single lock on the largest basin would
allow small craft access to the canal.

● *Manchester Evening News* journalist Chris Stewart and photographer Clive Cookson went along to cover the official opening ceremony of the £8million four-star Copthorne Hotel on Salford Quays, and watched as eleven-year-old Wayne Curran wormed his way through the crowd of more than 100 distinguished guests to see what all the fuss was about. Wayne put on his best grin for the photographers before he was whisked out of the picture by hotel staff.

● In April 1990 the big ships were back in Manchester Docks when this 1500 ton discharged a cargo of Portuguese timber in sight of the Salford Quays development. She was the first cargo ship to tie up at 1/9 dock since Manchester Liners axed its container service in 1984.

The World of Work

● In 1926, the country was in the grip of a general strike, and these people are doing what thousands of others were doing – surviving. Here women search a spoil heap at a local colliery hoping to find a little useable coal.

● Not so much about work as the lack of it. This picture, taken
by a *Manchester Evening News* photographer in December 1933,
shows a member of one of the Salvation Army mobile canteens
dishing out free coffee to unemployed men waiting outside the
labour exchange.

● When this picture was taken in 1970, the rag and bone man was an endangered species, and Charlie Rigby, who had at the time been in the business for thirty-five years, felt that it was getting harder by the day. "There aren't many of us left, and it's getting more and more difficult to make a living out of it."

Charlie's day started at 7.00am at his yard in Strawberry Road the first task being to feed and groom his horse before setting off on his round at about 8.00am. Rag and bone men each had their own patch and would not knowingly go into another's area.

● With only 11,104 miles on the clock, experimental gas-turbine locomotive GT3 is cut up during February 1966 at Tommy Ward's scrapyard in Ducie Road. Built by English Electric at Newton-le-Willows in 1961, GT3 was the culmination of 12 years work by a team of 15 engineers. Despite successful trials on BR, no orders were forthcoming as it was thought that this type of locomotive would prove too costly to operate.

● NCB Mosley Common Colliery in April 1967. When the National Coal Board was formed in 1947 there were twenty-two pits in the Manchester coalfield. Towards the end of the Second World War, Manchester Collieries had embarked on an ambitious scheme to completely rebuild the colliery. The NCB continued the programme which included widening the diameter of the main shaft by no less than 10ft and installing what was then the world's largest electric-driven winding engine.

● *MEN* photographer John Featherstone was despatched to NCB Agecroft Colliery, Pendlebury, on 5 January 1972, to take this picture of miners coming off the last shift prior to a national strike by the NUM in protest at a pay rise of just £2 a week by the NCB. By mid-February no less than fourteen power stations were off-line due to a lack of coal and the NUM disrupted supplies elsewhere with their effective use of around 15,000 flying pickets. The Conservative Government of the day declared a state of emergency and introduced a three-day week as power supplies were rationed.

● Rows of lamps line the racks in the miners' lamp room.

● Workers from Agecroft Colliery, Walkden, mount a 24-hour picket at Kearsley power station to stop any non-union oil deliveries.

● A policeman's helmet falls to the ground during a clash
with striking miners at Agecroft Colliery in May 1984.
Miners picketed at this Pendlebury colliery were striking as
part of the National Union of Mineworkers' strike 1984-85.

● Miners at Agecroft Colliery as they dismantle an electric motor in 1974. .

● The end of yet another era as Agecroft Colliery is demolished in September 1991.

● This is one of four 2-8-2 steam locomotives built at Nasmyth, Wilson & Co's Bridgewater Foundry, Patricroft, in 1935, for the Kiao Tsi Railway, China. The locomotive has been partially dismantled ready for transporting to the docks. It was quite normal for large steam locomotives to be sent in sections – on arrival they were usually reassembled on the dockside, fired up, and driven off.

● The sound of clogs of the cotton-mill workers on the cobblestones were once a part of everyday life. The wearing of clogs by mill workers was in terminal decline before the end of the Second World War and by 1950 there appears to have been only one clogmaker and repairer left, James Critchley, of Whit Lane, Salford. These girls were on strike when this picture was taken in August 1932.

This Sporting Life

- The paddock at Manchester racecourse on 31 May 1901, just before the big race – the Manchester Cup – won by J. Childs on Rambling Kate at 100-8. The following year the Manchester Cup was run on the new course at Castle Irwell as the New Barns course had been acquired by the Manchester Ship Canal Co for extensions to the docks.

● In June 1976, the *Manchester Evening News* broke the news that the owners of the Albion greyhound stadium at Lower Broughton had struck a private deal with Salford Corporation to sell the track for £300,000. The Albion was one of the first greyhound stadia to be opened in the country after the sport took off during the 1930s, but now the council had plans to build homes for 200 families on the 10.5 acre site on the banks of the Irwell.

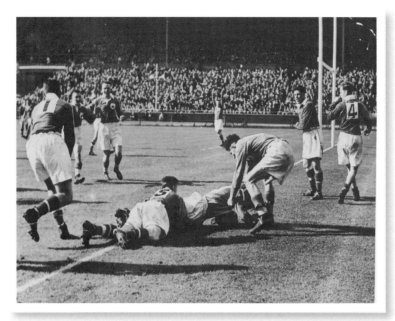

● Right centre, Albert Sear of Salford RLFC, scores the winning try against Barrow in the Rugby League Challenge Cup Final at Wembley on 7 May 1938.

● Gus Risman holds the 1938 Challenge Cup as he is chaired round the Wembley pitch. Bert Day is holding the base of the trophy and Dai Davies, on his right, is puffing away on a cigarette.

• Salford turns out to welcome the Red Devils home. During the mid to late thirties Salford were the most exciting, most glamorous side in Rugby League. The man at the front in the pork pie hat is Lance Todd, the team's legendary showman manager. Once again Gus Risman is the man with his hands on the silverware.

• The full line-up of Salford's 1938 Challenge Cup side. Back row (left to right) J. Feethman, D. M. Davies, H. W. Thomas, R. Brown, J. Bradbury. Third row (left to right) A. E. Edwards, P. Dalton, H. Osbaldestin, W. A. Williams, B. Hudson, H. C. Day, A. Gear. Second row (left to right) L. B. Todd (secretary-manager), C. B. Riley (chairman), A. J. Risman (capt), J. B. Goldstraw (vice-chairman), J. Dawson (trainer). Front row (left to right) S. E. Miller and W. Watkins.

● Jackie Brennan makes a pass during the 1969 Challenge Cup Final at Wembley gainst Castleford.

● Jonathan Quigley crashes through for a try during Salford's 30 – 13 away win over Warrington in November 1992.

● Salford RLFC line-up in August 1993 was, back row (left to right): Andy Burgess, Paul O'Neill, Steve Gibson, Shane Hansen, Scott Naylor, Ian Blease, Paul Forber and Peter Williams. Middle row (left to right): Darren Betts, Tony Howard, David Fell, Steve Blakeley, Wayne Reid, Ged Stazicker, David Young, John Gilfillan and Martin Birkett. Front row (left to right): Tex Evans, Jonathan Quigley, Gary Jack (player-manager), John Wilkinson (chairman), Howard Cartwright (coach), Mark Lee and Jason Critchley.

● Salford RLFC celebrate winning the Division One title in January 1996. This important win meant that the club were promoted into the newly formed Super League.

● Swinton RLFC in the 1880s. Nearby rivals Salford had been founded in 1879.

● The 1927-28 season Swinton RLFC with their haul of silverware: The Salford Royal Hospital Challenge Cup, the Northern Rugby Championship Cup, the Rugby League Challenge Cup, the Lancashire County Championship Cup, and the Lancashire County Challenge Cup.

● The Swinton RLFC side that lifted the 1963-64 league title to make it two in a row.

● Fire badly damaged the disused main stand, including offices and former function rooms at Swinton's Station Road headquarters in July 1992. The blaze was the latest in a series of vandal attacks at the club, which was moving out to share facilities with Bury Football Club at Gigg Lane. The team left Gigg Lane in 2002 and moved to within a mile of the Swinton and Pendlebury border, sharing Salford City's amateur football club's grounds at Moor Lane. There was a further move for the club in 2004 when they moved to Park Lane, Whitefield the home of Sedgley Park RUFC. In August 2006 the club acquired a lease on a piece of land bordering Swinton and Pendlebury. The club intends to build a stadium and finally bring the Lions team back to the home grounds.

● Swinton RLFC 1993-94 season. Back row (left to right) Tony Humphries, Ian Skeech, Stuart Turner, David Marsh, Andy Mikhail, Chris Ashurst, Adrian Erner, Chris Parr, Danny Whittle. Middle row (left to right) Tony Barrow (coach), Brian Best, Simon Ashcroft, Martin Leyland, Darrel Rogers, Paul Gartland, Mark Welsby, Barry Ledger, Richard Irving, Billy Benyon (assistant coach). Front row (left to right) Norman Brown (physio), Steve Entwistle, Colin Robinson, Gary Welsby, Ronnie Duane (capt), Paul Kay, Alex Melling and Steve Cunningham.

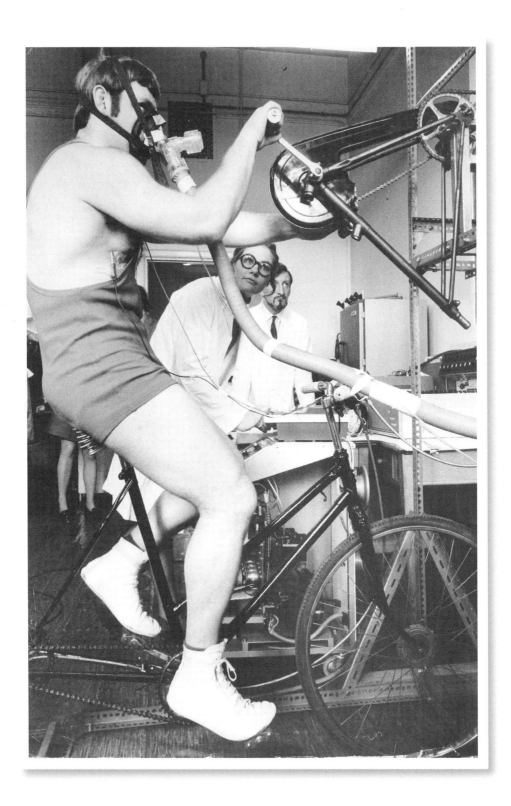

● The gentlemen of Peel Park Bowling Club show off their latest trophy.

● *Manchester Evening News* journalist Ann Sunderland went along to Salford University in April 1972 to see a new method of testing the fitness of Olympic wrestlers, devised by Dr. John Brooke, who was heading up the designated northern testing centre for the British Amateur Wrestling Association. Dr. Brooke's new machine, the ergowheel, was demonstrated by Richard Barraclough, a lecturer in physical education and member of the Olympic squad. The machine assessed fitness levels more effectively than before because it tested both arms and legs. The wrestler peddles one ergowheel with his feet and another with his hands. The oxygen mask measures the amount of oxygen used: the bigger the maximum oxygen uptake, the fitter the wrestler.

● Agecroft Rowing Club's maiden four on the
River Irwell on 29 July 1907.

● Watched by a large crowd of cheering students, Manchester
University completed their hat-trick over Salford when they
won the 1974 annual boat race over a mile-plus stretch
of the Irwell between Albert Bridge and Pomona Dock.The
Salford crew finished eighteen seconds behind their rivals.
But on the homeward stretch there was only half a length
between the two crews.

● The Boddington's Bitter University Boat Race between Salford and Manchester on May Bank Holiday 1995. Here both crews make their final preparations, with Manchester hoping for a smoother ride than they had in practice when their boat was damaged by submerged shopping trollies as they warmed up on the Bridgewater Canal.

● Dragon boat races at Salford Quays in July 1996.

Sponsors

A B Marsh Solicitors
Bodycote Testing Ltd
Business for Breakfast
Datum Group
Flue Stox
Homesales Consultants Ltd
Hamburg Süd
Lee's Motors

A B Marsh Solicitors

A B Marsh Solicitors started business in January 1998 on Deansgate, before they moved to Bexley Square in Salford in June 1998. An area famed for the Battle of Bexley Square, it was outside the Town Hall in 1931 that police and local unemployed Salford workers clashed during a demonstration.

Bexley Square is the home of Salford Magistrates Court, the perfect location for a firm of solicitors.

However, needing bigger premises, *A B Marsh* moved to Chapel Walks in August 2006 into newly refurbished offices within the arches under the Salford Central to Manchester Victoria railway line on Chapel Street. The railway line and arches were built in 1843, and the arches have now been modernised combining Victorian architecture with a contemporary urban feel.

AB Marsh initially specialised in criminal law, dealing with some very serious and high profile cases since they started practicing. In recent times the company

has expanded to offer family law, conveyancing services, wills and probate.

Preserving an individual identity is important to *A B Marsh*, and they pride themselves on maintaining a personal and professional approach with clients.

Bodycote Testing Group

Bodycote Testing Group is part of Bodycote International Plc, one of the world's largest independent providers of testing and thermal processing services.

The company has a rich 70-year history and although they were not founded in the city of Salford, their roots are synonymous with Salford's industrial heritage. As textile manufacturers, they became market leaders across Europe after many strategic acquisitions.

The decline of the textile industry at the end of the 1970s saw *Bodycote* make the decision to leave textiles behind and focus on a new services-led business. Their strategy was to acquire various heat treatment and metallurgical testing companies, which would allow them to expand their portfolio as well as their global presence.

Bodycote Testing Group has 38 locations in the UK and over 100 locations

worldwide. They acquired their brand new, purpose-built premises in Centenary Park to house its North West materials testing and Pipeline Development businesses. Centenary Park is a prestigious new development in Eccles, located adjacent to Trafford Park.

The new facility also provides a base for a number of the *Bodycote Testing Group* directors as well as training facilities to serve the company across Europe. Councillor Valerie Burgoyne, the Mayor of Salford, officially opened the new laboratory and offices in June 2007.

Testing of materials, components and other derivatives is a crucial necessity for many industries. It ensures that quality is controlled, products are validated and specifications are complied with. Using their skilled workforce and state-of-the-art technology, the *Bodycote Testing Group* can offer a testing service to their clients that is second to none.

Datum Group

The city of Salford grew through industrialisation; cloth and silk were produced in abundance while the bleaching and dyeing processes were prevalent in the town. For this reason, along with the opening of the Manchester Ship Canal, Salford became one of the richest cotton towns and brought employment to the area for nearly a century.

Swinton was famous for its industrial school, which closed in the 1920s when the site was used in 1938 to build the impressive town hall. With local government changes and the formation of the new city of Salford in 1974, Swinton's central position and its town hall saw it become the official administrative headquarters of Salford.

Datum Group, a specialist recruitment company, were formed in 2000 with offices on Moorside Road in Swinton. Owner Stuart Law has been in the recruitment industry since 1989, forming his own businesses and

working at Director level with numerous leading recruitment specialists throughout the country. Today Datum Personnel, part of the *Datum Group* are a successful recruitment business focusing on a niche and specialist

market. They supply voice and data communication engineers to technical companies, a business sector that is experiencing substantial growth in today's high-tech environment. With the redevelopment of Salford and the

birth of many new urban apartments, Stuart Law has embraced a new business opportunity. In 2006 Time & Space was set up as a separate company to complement today's contemporary lifestyle by offering domestic support services such as ironing, cleaning, shopping and dog walking.

Caxton Hall
Chapel Street, Salford

Caxton Hall, Chapel Street was originally built in 1907 for the Manchester Typographical Association, a union of printer workers. The building's links with the printing industry is how the building came to have its name. The members of the Typographical Association held William Caxton, the man who standardised usage of the English language and developed printing in the UK in 1476, in high regard.

Before the construction of *Caxton Hall*, the members of the Typographical Association were involved with the Socialist Movement in Manchester. They were influential in the formation of the Manchester and Salford Trades Council and were instrumental in organising a group of Unions to meet at the Mechanics Institute in 1868, regarded as the first recorded TUC meeting.

Caxton Hall became the venue for many Socialist and Labour meetings thereafter. The hall has also born witness to many wartime debates as well as hosting the Communist Party's Ninth Annual Congress.

Homesales Consultants Ltd

Homesales Consultants Ltd are based in Caxton Hall and provide mortgage and insurance advice. This is a much-needed service in the rapidly changing property market.

The company is a mortgage consultancy, able to deal with any mortgage lender, best suited to the clients needs. They have been based in Caxton Hall for over ten years, under the management of David Mullin. Prior to taking over the company in 1996 he was a partner in a similar business for over twenty years.

In the current financial climate, with the ever changing criteria required by mortgage lenders, the advice which Homesales Consultants Ltd offer, is invaluable to anyone who needs to arrange a mortgage.

Flue Stox

During the development of Salford Quays many of the new roads were named after American States to commemorate the five month long tour in 1887 by the legendary Buffalo Bill and his troupe of buffalos, broncos and Native Americans, including members of the infamous Sioux tribe. They based their camp by the River Irwell in Salford and performed their Wild West shows to sell out crowds at Salford and Manchester's Belle Vue.

Today Salford Quays still retains several avenues with American connections, for example Ohio, Michigan, Dakota and Kansas.

Nearly one hundred years later, in 1986, *Flue Stox* built premises at Boston Court on Kansas Avenue. Owner Colin Taylor formed the business in 1981 and *Flue Stox* is now a specialist distributor of flue pipes and chimneys.

The company continues to expand its portfolio and has become merchants of stainless steel sanitary products.

Hamburg Süd

When the Manchester Ship Canal opened in 1894, Furness Withy was one of the principal shipping companies that used the Port of Manchester.

Christopher Furness, of Furness Withy, started a trial in 1897 to sail ships from Salford to Montreal. A dedicated shipping line for this service was supported and funded by Furness Withy, Manchester Ship Canal Company and the Canadian Government, amongst other investors.

By 1898 the company Manchester Liners was formed and at its helm was Chris Furness as Chairman and main shareholder. The appointed Managing Director was Robert Burdon Stoker, who also worked for Furness Withy.

As a subsidiary of Furness Withy, Manchester Liners saw three generations of Burdon Stokers take control of the business. During Furness Withy's history they had over 1,000 ships in their fleet including the prestigious Royal Mail Line, and at times this was the largest fleet in the world. During both World Wars ships were lost from the fleet, but the company rebuilt, repaired and re-sailed.

By the end of the 1960s Manchester Liners operated Britain's first fully cellular vessel from the docks at Salford to Montreal and also ran a direct container service between Salford and the Great Lakes of Canada. The company expanded to offer services such as ship repairs, container repairs and port management. It was at this time that Manchester Liners had new premises built in Salford, appropriately named Manchester Liners House, the building shaped like a ship's bridge. Still visible on the Salford skyline, the building is more commonly known as Furness House.

Manchester Liners moved their operations to Ellesmere Port in the 1970s as ship sizes grew with the increased popularity of container services. Being part of the Furness Group, they were bought out by Orient Overseas Container Holdings of Hong Kong in 1980.

In 1990 the German international container shipping company *Hamburg Süd* acquired the Furness Withy business. A world leading carrier, on the North – South trade routes, their *Hamburg Süd's* UK operations run from Salford's Furness House, at the head of the ship canal, where it all began for Furness Withy and Manchester Liners.

Lee's Motors

The Exchange train station closed in 1969. It once boasted the longest passenger platform in the world but suffered severe bomb damage during the Second World War.

Today, beneath the arches of the platform and Chapel Street lies New Kings Head Yard, next to the site of the former Kings Head public house. The famous writer and businesswoman, Elizabeth Raffald moved and took ownership of the pub in 1773 with her husband John Raffald. She was famed for teaching her domestic and culinary skills to other women as well as writing famous works such as "The Experienced English Housekeeper" and the "Directory of Manchester".

The area once formed part of Greengate, the one time historical core of Salford, where markets and fairs were in abundance. However with the industrial decline the area became dilapidated and land was under used.

In 1971 Martin Lee, the proprietor of Lee's Motors who arrived in this country in the mid 1960s as a teenager, started trading in Salford as a repair workshop. In the 1980s small repair garages were being pushed out by main dealers and insurance companies. This led to Martin diversifying into car parking.

Over the years Martin has managed to acquire most of the arches beneath the Exchange station along Chapel Street, from Deal Street to Victoria Street including the appoach road leading up to the long platform. Such expansion led Martin to offer approximately 1,100 parking spaces.

In recent times some of the spaces have been lost to development, but there are a considerable amount left.

Martin's secure facilities and on-site valet services are appreciated by his regulars: both corporate and visitors alike. Martin has also operated car parks on the site of the now Trinity footbridge, the Lowry Hotel and the new Inland Revenue building on Chapel Street.

Maintenance & Rewind Services

Maintenance & Rewind Services have supplied maintenance and engineering products including bearings, power transmission products, hand tools, power tools, safety clothing and apparel since 1999.

Based at industrial premises on Bright Road, Eccles, a town enriched with a history of silk, cotton and steel production since the early 1800s.

Bearings have been integral throughout engineering history, they allow motors and wheels to spin smoothly and quietly. Without them parts would be regularly worn out through friction and would need constant replacement.

The first bearings were made of wood and were used in water mills for cooling and lubrication. In 1898 Henry Timken, an innovator in the manufacture of carriages, patented the first tapered roller bearing.

A year later he formed his own company who today are one of the largest bearing manufacturers in the world. *Maintenance & Rewind Services* supply Timken, FAG and SKF bearings for their clients.

Maintenance & Rewind Services have a variety of customers from transport to logistics companies and printing houses to food factories.

Business for Breakfast

Business for Breakfast started in 2000 when some families from Eccles came together to generate ideas for improved sales. As the meetings became more regular, word of mouth saw more local business representatives attend the meetings, and as a result a networking group was formed. Offering a more informal and relaxed approach to the business deal, the networking meetings became increasingly popular and were held regularly at hotels such as the Marriott hotel in Worsley.

John Fisher with his wife Mel acquired their Peel Street premises in Eccles in 2003, and at the same time started a franchise for the business. As the popularity of their morning business network meetings grows, *Business for Breakfast* have made rapid expansion throughout the south of the country, and are now rolling out the meetings internationally.

free internet access . family history . talking books . business information . talks . art . homework centres . language courses . theatre . help for inventors . DVDs . free events for kids . festivals . silver surfer clubs . local images collection . bestsellers . author visits . CDs . free computing courses . newspapers . mobiles . community information . brilliant books . displays . on-line learning . reading groups . CD-ROMs . culture . local history . books for babies . exhibitions . advice . workshops . live poetry . sheet music . what's on . treasures . coffee . videos . storytimes . fun

When did you last visit your library?

www.manchester.gov.uk/libraries

MANCHESTER
CITY COUNCIL

Other Manchester titles also available

ISBN 9781-84547-092-0 £14.99

ISBN 9781-84547-117-0 £12.99

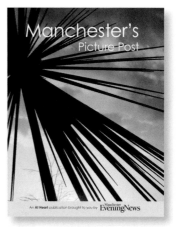

ISBN 9781-84547-107-1 £16.99

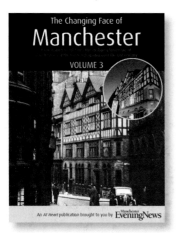

ISBN 9781-84547-160-6 £12.99

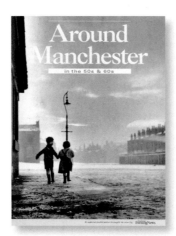

ISBN 9781-904038-19-0 £9.99

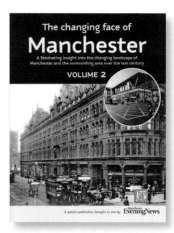

ISBN 9781-84547-104-0 £14.99

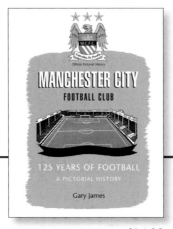

ISBN 9781-84547-103-3 £14.99

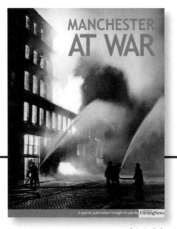

ISBN 9781-84547-096-8 £14.99

These books are available from all good bookshops
or alternatively call AtHeart on: 0161 924 0159